CW00857758

Towards A Distant Horizon

Horizon

(Rambling all the Way)

By :Andrew Siddle

CONTENTS

CONTENTS

Introduction

Introduction

This is the fourth volume of my poems that have been published. Once again full of random comments, and observations, within each poem introduction. Towards a Distant Horizon! It means looking to the future and building on the past instead of drowning in the depths of yesterday's muddy puddles! Some humorous poetry and some sad. Some in rhyme and some in popular prose poetry style. A poetic future built from a rich solid tapestry of history, folklore, and style from yesterday. Enjoy reading it!

A Welcome to Spring

A Welcome to Spring

When I first started to decide on which order the poems in this book should go; I couldn't make my mind up which poem to start the book with. Then I thought "Towards a new horizon, new beginnings, a new destiny?" what would that be? Well "new beginnings" are synonymous with the new growth of little green stems pushing up through the soil in spring time. So I decided to start the book with a spring time poem. Here it is!

A Welcome to Spring

Sing low dear friend,

let the weariness of winter now fall away,

whistle your time till the buds rise and break to spring time fun,

green stems sway and bow to your low pitched tune.

Sing low and watch the green man scatter his seed,

the seed of new growth under the watchful gaze of his steady eye.

Daffodils spring forth from their lifeless beds,

gently tossing their pillows aside.

Growing stronger with each new smile,

getting bigger with each new born day.

Watch for the Snow Drops and let the pansies grin once more,

smiling at the sun as only they know how,

oh how the clouds and the wind pass by.

Sing low old friend let your breeze now cover my face,

another morning and another day,

let the sun now guide the way,

so let spring begin.

New Beginnings

New Beginnings

Some people in life take the view that one must take what ever is granted, as one's lot, and then be satisfied with that which is given. In my experience life is mostly a fake experience; because mankind are in charge of who gets what and mankind are inherently corrupt. Our experiences in life, and what we have , are generated by the way that we react and interreact with other human beings.

Everything is changeable, and everything is generated by society and mankind. For every person viewing the beautiful dawn sun rise there is another person planning on how to rip that person off and steal from them. Such is life. In fact that is life!

What ever people get out of life is generated , by other people, because everything in society is generated by mankind. So if you are not happy with your lot in life just go out and get something better for yourself. You can do it and it can be done. We are not talking about money necessarily; just satisfaction with life and quality of life here.

New Beginnings

Fresh breeze in the morning's glow,

take to the air with summer's flow,

then head on to a vista new,

flow with the breeze and follow true.

Follow the breeze to a distant place,

take the air with the sun on your face,

just disappear without a fear,

a call from afar; an oasis clear.

A call from afar to a distant hill,

far from this known old place here still,

and the call is deep within my blood,

as wanderlust is understood.

I still yearn to chase the breeze,

in summer's height beyond these trees,

and places new I've yet to know,

just pack and leave with inner glow.

So new beginnings yet beyond,

far from the place I once was fond,

as yearnings grow to follow the breeze,

and "come now" whisper the rustling trees.

A Call to Life

A Call to Life

A call to life is about grasping your opportunities before they decay. It is about ensuring that one recognises, and takes up, every chance in life that is available to one personally. If chances are not recognised then life starts to decline without having ever achieved anything. That being the case a lifetime has been wasted.

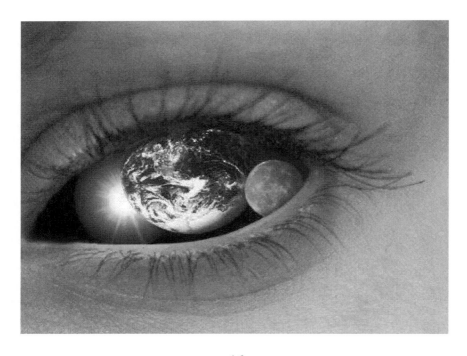

A Call to Life

For the flower blooms but for a while,

as youth and love reveal a smile,

a smile at jest and youthful style,

a time for all who run the mile.

Then when the mile is run and passed.

nought but memories now last,

so cast your seed and spread it all,

as time and space will not recall.

Your page in life is all but set,

from day of birth that's what you'll get,

so shirk not with all doubts that call,

your mind must clear or you may fall.

Grasp each chance that comes your way,

or lead your life in times decay,

a glowing orb by planets fled,

but once then gone it's time was said.

Life is set and life is great,

but wait not for your time so late,

each new morning passing by,

one day less beneath the sky.

The Roamin' Road

The Roamin' Road

The Roamin' road! That's the one for me. The open highway to somewhere or other. Doesn't matter where 'cause there are always new things to see. One could spend a lifetime travelling around the world and still not know every single bit. Split between a property profession career , and earlier work as an external armed intelligence agent, to SIS/MI6, I have done a fair wee tad of travel for work reasons. The western Sahara in Africa, Morocco of the Barbary Coast - North Africa, Scotland, The Nevada Desert in the USA, France, Spain, Italy, New York City in the USA. All over the place. I wouldn't have it any other way. Travel is good for the soul and for breaking down barriers between different people and different cultures.

The Roamin' Road

Life's cut short when a man's hemmed in,

no where to go and a bottle of gin,

who ever said a Tiger would stay and just sit,

when the road winds on for a traveller to hit.

Roads of the distance are a man's place to be,

never stay long there are places to see,

a man wasn't made to sit on a couch,

with a beer gut diction and a permanent slouch.

So the village on the hill top is where I'll be gone,

and even when there I will not stay long,

for the world is so wide and the oceans so deep,

don't cage me in my soul you shan't keep.

Weep will I not for the places that I leave,

time travels on and these dusty roads heave,

as the Heavens bake the tarmac with the midday sun,

get my bags packed there is travel to be done.

<u>Sun Rise</u>

Sun Rise

Just a little cinquain for a change here. Dedicated to a sunny sun shine morning. What could be better?

* Cinquain poems must be 5 lines long.

* A Cinquain poem has 2 syllables on the first line, 4 on the second, 6 on the third, 8 on   the 4th, and 2 syllables on the 5th line.

* Cinquain poems do not need to rhyme but can if you want.

<u>Sun Rise</u>

Sun rise,

spray us with gold,

aura of light to all,

warmth and brightness for all to share,

as one.

Rainy Day Spring

Rainy Day Spring

Well now; what better way to spend a rainy morning in spring than sit writing a poem about a rainy morning in spring? So that's what I did do! Spring is my favourite time of year because winter drives me spare. Hate it. I always look forward to my little friends the buds of spring! Here the lads come again. Uncurling and shooting up their little green stems.

Rainy Day Spring

Rainy days they come and go,

though clouds are grey and soon will go,

and water droplets splash the ground,

in little prisms all is found.

Primroses now open wide,

dripping splash in all I find,

and daffodils that bow their heads,

sleepy rainy times in bed.

Magnolia buds that fill up high,

from the window where I spy,

and soon to open where they spread,

their blossom canopy is bred.

Water butts now fill to burst,

and ratta tat from gutter thirst,

gulping all the rain to come,

as road sides pool till all is done.

Each drop of rain brings forth a flower,

each drop of rain exerts a power,

each ratta tat wakes up a seed,

and bulbs burst forth and start to feed.

Oh spring time turn the seasons round,

so wake the spirit from the ground,

Pansies come and Lilies sit,

green shoots sprout and start to fit.

Let me feel primordial glow,

shine from all about to grow,

that ancient feel of start to life,

as all now oust old winter's strife.

See me smile as blossoms bud,

Cherry high in pink set hood,

Camellia white and pushing through,

for all creation's work is true.

Marigolds that look sublime,

Mountain Laurel all in time,

Orchids shout and wave their hands,

and Tulips know of all these plans.

City Vibe

City Vibe

I've always said that , personally, I have two modes of
existence style wise. I can fit right in the heart of the
inner city. Or I can fit in the countryside. I don't have
a half way house of style that allows me to be part of
what we call small town culture. I'm either City
centre or rural. That is not to say I have anything
against small town people. It's just that I can't do it
because small town style isn't my style. Anyway;
thought I'd do a city vibe poem just to keep it "cool" !

City Vibe

In my mind the city lights,
music beats and street life heights,
far away from work time strife,
now here I am for street time life.

Beat born babe now hits the floor,
denim clad she knows the score,
she hits the beat while some look on,
cast in denim beat time gone.

Strobe lights frisk the dance floor highs,
reds and golds they light from nigh,
mirrored walls and Bangla bass,
chat her friendly draw the ace.

Lager glasses clank as one,
whisky Mac the Vodka's gone,
bar snacks crunch till there are none,
dance club feeling starts to throng.

Hands in air and foot kick bass,
all go crazy fill the space,
dance floor lit while dudes hi five,
loudest music aint no dive.

Outside now the taxis come,
trend set dress or you they'll shun,
so what is trendy or what is dull,
passing through before they're full.
So set me up and dazzle strong,

deep beneath the strobe light long,
dancing vibes and all as one,
beat time see that all belong.

City lights I saw your name,
winding streets of city fame,
high rise windows dark outside,
darkened skies and sights to prize.

Let the buzz now set me free,
city life's the night time key,
leads me on to deep felt breadth,
way inside such culture's depth.

The Rise of the Prell

The Rise of the Prell

What exactly are the Prell? Well I'm not sure exactly but they are probably an invented species of night time monster that I invented one late evening. Probably after a glass of wine or maybe I was just feeling bored. ;)

The Rise of the Prell

The Prell they pang for the Yin Tang Doe,

tis true,

tis true.

Bellowing cries and jab jib dees,

weak knees

weak knees.

Rising from flatland copse they come,

they soar,

they soar.

Flapping their jargabs and anger in dops,

they dive,

they dive.

Hide small one for they see your way,

you flee,

you flee.

Following on they screech and see,

you reach,

you reach.

slamming your door you hide inside,

you stay,

you stay.

But the Prell swarm round on multiple sides,

you scream,

you scream.

So trapped indoors both dream and real,

they swoop,

they swoop.

You wake from a dream but they screech high and low,

tis real,

tis real.

With dawn they are gone to the realm of beyond,

new day,

new day.

But beware the Prell and avoid what they say,

be gone,

be gone.

The church bells toll for the rising day,

tis gone,

tis gone.

Worship the hours as morning has come,

so start,

so start.

Give praise for the day and the morning sun,

your heart,

so start.

And call not the Prell for they surely will come,

you're young,

tis done.

The Ostrich Inn

The Ostrich Inn

This is the tale of the Ostrich Inn which is in Colnbrook in Buckinghamshire. The Inn was founded in the 12th century but still operates in 2018. Back in time it was run by a couple called John and Mary Jarman. Not content with just serving customers with hearty ale, good food, and a bed for the night these hosts took up the habit of murdering their guests. This was by a clever trap door placed under a bed in one of the guest rooms which was operated by a lever and cable system. Mr and Mrs Jarman used to get wealthy guests drunk then drop them through the floor, whilst sleeping in bed, into a vat of boiling ale in a room below the bedroom. Over a period of time they murdered and robbed 59 guests at the Inn.

The Ostrich Inn

In centuries gone by there was an Inn,
such a darkest secret was the Ostrich sin,
the pub they called the Ostrich Inn,
Medieval place and darkest sin.

Run by the Jarmans in bygone days,
many guests arrived and many stayed,
for every now and then was found,
some of the guests made not a sound.

So many guests came and slept so sound,
but sometimes one went to the ground,
and now and then and oh so blind,
a number of guests could no one find?

For the Jarmans ran a fair old trade,
with cash and wallets and stolen braid,
the finest cloaks and necklaces too,
they killed the lot for this wealth so true.

When the wealthiest guests begot so drunk,
a trap door opened and there they sunk,
to a boiling vat of ale below,
and pickled guest in ale did flow.

59 dropped down from their beds,
at night time drunk and out of their heads,
to that vat of boiling ale below,
and their money taken to the Jarmans glow.

59 guests there lost a life,
dropped through a trap in drunken strife,
and years went by till the Jarmans were caught,
with loveliest treasures from the dead they'd caught.

But once found they swung their final hour,
called time at the Inn did the Jarmans Cower?
cower at the call to the gallows pole,
and there to be hung so lost their soul.

Swinging from rope of the gallows taught,
so ended this drunken death trap sort,
swinging with the breeze from left to right,
while the crows beyond all called in might.

Walter's Weather Warning.

Walter's Weather Warning.

Well I've seen so many weather forecasts , on the television, that I can even remember when Michael Fish fist started on BBC television news weather. Does it really matter though? So long as we get some sort of weather does it matter what type of weather we get? That's more or less what this poem is about.

Walter's Weather Warning.

Watch out for the weather said Walter Kay,
wither the weather in the month of May,
though whether the weather be withered or not,
watch out for the weather and dither fair not.

Don't dither or slither when the weather comes round,
weather endeavours to be all around,
and whether tis good or whether tis bad,
beware the weather or you'll be so sad.

In April the weather was mostly here,
weathered and tethered to March's fear,
but whether it's June or January's time,
beware the weather in every clime.

The weather is clever and all should know,
watch how it dawdles and sometimes goes slow,
then changes so quickly and fast as a flash,
the weather goes faster as if in a dash.

Always beware of the weather at night,
and in the daytime beware how it can fight,
rough or smooth it is weather for sure,
if you don't want weather there's really no cure.

When I was young we had weather a lot,
and some times sat and watched what we'd got,
for the weather was there almost every day,
so watch the weather that's all I will say.

The weather abroad is always there,
at holiday time and people do share,
weather is cool but sometimes so hot,
a sky full of weather is all that we've got.

Weather up north and weather down south,
weather aint fussy just ask our old Alf,
once we had weather almost every day.
we couldn't do nothing and there it did stay.

Weather is big but sometimes so small,
sometimes at sea it's loudest of all,
then sometimes on land there's hardly a sound,
nice little weather in all that we've found.

So Walter announces for the Radio Tay,
"today we have weather and here it will stay",
whether tis withered or whether tis good,
beware the weather and all understood!

<u>He's Going Bodmin</u>

He's Going Bodmin

Bodmin is a civil Parish and historic town in Cornwall. However it is Bodmin Moor that is the more famous. With very wild landscapes, the remnants of mines from previous centuries, and agricultural small holdings traditionally miles from humanity. In modern Cornish street culture "going Bodmin" means to go mad. As in "Our Jake's goin' Bodmin innit?" This being on the basis of the solitude and loneliness of some of the Bodmin Moor agricultural smallholdings. There again "going Bodmin" also means to visit a beautiful and in some ways unspoilt Moorish terrain in Cornwall.

He's Going Bodmin

Cairns of stones mirrored the way,
by fields of wild grass, and trees, and hay,
and horses so wild that they scatter on sight,
of all those who approach be it day or night.

Where's our Joe then,
old Jack did shout,
Oh he's gone Bodmin,
he 's gone right out.

With Fowey of the upland high,
silhouetted up against the sky,
and scattered ruins of old tin mines,
the remnants of our oldest times.

Where's our Lucy then,
old Jack did shout,
oh she's gone Bodmin,
she's gone right out.

A tin mine there in the fields,
ruins of all at once reveals,
like some castle in the flowing rain,
a remnant of what was once so plain.

Where's our Pete then,
old Jack did say,
oh he's gone Bodmin,
he's gone right out.

The river Tiddy "ogged" it's way,
round by Lynher in it's sway,
and flowing close to Tamar too,
while Camel passed the gentle few.

Where's our Kate then,
old Jack did shout,
oh she's gone Bodmin,
she's gone right out.

So river Warleggan was there as well,
flowing steady and full of swell,
and river Inny crossed beyond,
by the moors of which we are so fond.

Where's old Ned then,
old Jack did shout,
oh he's gone Bodmin,
he's gone right out.

With grey stone walls so dryly laid,
and a little cottage in which we stayed,
the granite Tors that wave to the peak,
as crossing fields wild beauty we seek.

I think I'm away then,
Old Jack did shout,
I'm going Bodmin,
but everyone was out.

The Age of Aquarius

The Age of Aquarius

The age of Aquarius started in 2011/2012. It marked the end of a previous astrological period of a little over two thousand years presided over by Pisces. Each astrological age adds up to an aggregated total of a little over 26,000 years of time. The final house to enter is the twelfth before we are supposed to return to our original position as the planet Earth. This obviously assumes perfection of all orbiting stars , planets and constellations. There will be a time when it will not be possible to return to the first house astral position any more. Each individual astrological age is just over two thousand years and there are twelve astrological houses to get through before the whole system resets back to the very first house again. At present as we enter the 2160, or so, years of the Age of Aquarius we are entering the seventh house. The gravitational forces, at play, during each astrological period are said to affect the way that human beings think and this is why each dominant house produces different dominant personality traits within human beings as one house changes to another. This works in the same way that the gravitational pull of the moon affects a woman's monthly menstrual cycle and decides when her period will be. Or another example ; the high tide of a sea is determined by the position of the moon and it's gravitational pull. The planets also exert a gravitational pull which does similar things to us on earth (in theory...obviously we don't know about reality!).

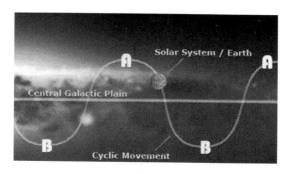

The Age of Aquarius

A New Age and a new time I guess. As Pisces descended so Aquarius rose. Rose to a new slow conversion of thoughts and time and; change? A new notion and a new way to be? Who knows!

2012 was the day it came. That slow slow conversion of thought and notion and space. So they say! They say " a new dawn of high technology culture and information sharing " what ever that is! A death of autocracy as a culture of information sharing grows. Who am I to argue?

Beyond belief to some. Maybe to me. 2160 years of a new Aquarian ethos. So what ethos would it be? Sharing of ideas, Sharing of thoughts, new technologies, and new information systems? Maybe!

A rise of high technological development beyond our wildest dreams? Maybe? Is it real or is it just in the unconscious dreams of a group of astrologists?

The end of autocracy and a New age of shared responsibilities, shared information technologies, new innovation as well. An end to autocracy?

Too good to be true or a real New Age? We have 2000 years of it to decide which. The years will show and time will tell I guess. The years will show. The years will show something I guess.

Lyonesse Revisited

Lyonesse Revisited

Lyonesse, or Lethowstow as Local Cornish would say, is the area of land that finally collapsed between the Cornish Coast and the Isles of Scilly. It is also the area of land that was intensely mined for tin for centuries and centuries. It was probably the level of mass undermining of the land whilst extracting tin that led to the eventual collapse of the whole area which fell under the waves. Some have suggested that the final battle between Arthur and Mordred may have been on this now vanished area of land. The area of land that disappeared would have been 30 miles in in length and covered the majority of what would have been Arthurian lands.

Lyonesse Revisited

When time was young there was a land,
on Albion's scene both green and planned,
with fields and hills and streams to the sea,
and orchards lush with apples free.
The sun it shone and the wind it blew,
and the days and nights of time just flew,
so Lyonesse the finest of all,
the pearl of Albion and pride at it's core.
Castles and knights of hill top peaks,
and sea gulls flew by with fish in their beaks,
Between Scilly and the rugged coast,
lie all that is left ; the Lyonesse ghost,
deep beneath the wild waves blue,
lie stone walls of fields and the last of the few.
For Lyonesse fell to the evilest tide,
and Albion's loss was Danu's pride.
Taken from man to the depths of the blue
and there she lies for all time true.
Here once fought Mordred and Arthur of old,
this land now drowned where they were so bold,
orchards and hills and church bells that rang,
buried way down where the Herring so swam.

The Robin

The Robin

We feed the birds out in the back garden. So every morning , from about 6am onwards, we have a load of them squawking, squabbling, and frantic scurrying. Very rarely see a robin but once every now and then there is one. So I thought I'd dedicate this next poem to the chap.

The Robin

A robin landed on my sill,
his heart it fluttered there until,
his regal robes and reddest vest,
surely showed of birds he's best.

Oh Robin tell me of the world,
and all your travels now unfurled,
what see you of all our plight?
Flying by with all your might?

Yet here you perch and look at me,
and all alone but yet so free,
the anger of the wildest beast,
would surely lay down at your feet.

For in your solitude you see,
the beauty of the wild born free,
and in your eye I see it shine,
an echo of a distant time,
when all creation came as new,
and you were born of all the few.

Now take to flight dear Robin do,
and fly your lonely path so true,
sometimes I look at you so free,
and watch awhile whilst in your tree.

The Epic of Pwyll of Dyfed

The Epic of Pwyll of Dyfed

Pwyll was an ancient Prince of Dyfed in Wales. Pwyll Pendefig Dyfed is a legendary tale from medieval Welsh literature and the first of four branches of the Mabinogi. It is about the friendship between the Prince of Dyfed and Arawn who is Lord of Annwn (Pronounced Anween) which is the otherworld/underworld.

This epic is part of the tale of Pwyll Pendefig Dyfed but does not include the birth and dissapearance of Pryderi who was son of Pwyll and his wife Rhiannon later on.

The Epic of Pwyll of Dyfed

Pwyll and the hunt

The morn drew swiftly to the sound of a horn,
a sound that summoned the hunt to be born,
and all came around grouped on the green,
warriors and knights and lords to be seen.

From the green set they to a distant copse,
gallops and cries and the wind never stops,
so there at the front rode proudly our Pwyll,
early dew risings and hooting of owl.

Taking the rough with a high jump in style,
jumping the bracken they started to smile,
but then in the distance the strangest of sounds,
a circle of barking manic hunt hounds.

The Prince called his huntsmen to gather and see,
strange hounds circled twixt tree lines so free,
and there in their midst a newly killed hog,
the hounds barked and gnarled while they ate in the
fog.

In fury Pwyll rode and drove them away,
then called on his own hounds to feed there that day,
so there now these Welsh hunt hounds of the Prince,
took over the feast and ate all they'd seen since.

Not till later did Pwyll then find,
the hounds he chased were somebody's pride,
the pride of Arawn Lord of those under,
and when he found out Lord Arawn did thunder,

shouting and screaming that his hounds had lost,

and wanting revenge at any true cost.

The Treaty of Pwyll and Arawn.

Now Arawn was known to all those around,
proud of his hounds that Pwyll had found,
and proud of his own hunting esteem,
Lord was he of the dark unseen.

Lord of the underworld and their king,
below the earth it belonged to him,
still in order to try to keep the peace,
Arawn agreed that all rage should cease.

In recompense for Pwyll's deed,
of chasing the hounds of Arawn from feed,
Arawn agreed to change his place,
and live as Pwyll as was the case.

Then Pwyll in order to stay a friend,
in his place Pwyll would descend,
to be Lord of the otherworld below,
King of the dark unseen as known.

For one year he would rule the dead,
lost souls below with he as head,
then in one year they both would meet,
Arawn again to take his seat.

In one year both would meet,
and tell their tales and truly greet,
then change right back upon the call,
with Pwyll in charge of Dyfed all.

Arrival of Rhiannon

Upon the return of Phyll to Wales,
many rejoiced with most hearty ales,
and in the fields the sun did shine,
the straw and the wheat both swayed in time.

Then through the distant wooded glade,
rode out a lady robed with braid,
and as her long hair flowed behind,
her face it seemed so pure and kind.

Her horse it cantered through the trees,
then on beyond bright buzzing bees,
and all the flowers bowed as one,
to see and greet this lady young.

So there she was Rhiannon so free,
this lady wild and pure was she,
and down flowed folds of braided gold,
as her horse rode on through field and road.

The wedding of Pwyll and Rhiannon

After seeing Rhiannon two hearts were entwined,
besotted was Pwyll and so they pined,
and later that day went on one knee,
pleading to Rhiannon so bonded was she,
marriage proposed with a goblet of wine,
two hearts grow bold with oneness in time.

Just then in the morn came a stranger from far,
dressed in black and marked with a scar,
and though the wedding and feast day were nigh,
the stranger asked Pwyll a favour to try.

Being joyous at the thought of his wedding day kiss,
Pwyll said yes I vow to do this,
the man then reveals to be Gwawl ap Clud,
and Pwyll's heart sank down with a thud.

For Gwawl now demanded Rhiannon for his,
as his wife now for the vow shall be this,
stupid Pwyll felt such a fool,
but vow would he however so cruel.

So gave up Rhiannon to Gwawl did he,
and a wedding day set for one year for she,
to be wed to Gwawl ap Clud on that day,
reluctant but faithful to Clud would she stay.

So the wedding to Pwyll was lost for that day,

though the guests still came and ate well away,
splendid was all in the feast laid before,
though no wedding they dined as never before.

The Defeat of Gwawl ap Clud

Now Pwyll was sad at the loss of his wife,
and clever was he in causing some strife,
one year now passed since the visit from Gwawl,
and loyal to his vow Pwyll plotted in style.

Seeking advice from the wizard of Annwn,
a present for Pwyll brought to be seen,
to the court of Pwyll in Dyfed for free,
a present of magic to win as key,
and the present was a bag of cloth so black.
A magic bag for to win his wife back,

Now when one year had passed and the wedding day
ready,
Pwyll took Rhiannon to Gwawl so steady,
and so sure of magic to trick Gwawl ap Clud,
so there he asked Gwawl of what he would?

If I ask a favour of you for to vow?
then Gwawl said "well; if reasoned I shall",
so Pwyll requested his black bag be filled,
full up with food to be shared as he willed.

" Fill my black bag with food to take home"

" And Rhiannon is yours ; for you alone!"

So Gwawl ap Clud agreed at once,
and started to fill the bag in response,
but the bag being magic could never be filled,
and crying and screaming Gwawl was to be killed.
For the bag opened wider and swallowed Gwawl
down,
the echo of screams made the court frown,
so Pwyll tied up the black bag with string,
and the knights all around stamped on this thing.
Till nothing was left of Gwawl ap Clud,
then the bag with it's magic burst with a thud,
to thunder and lightning and the guards of Annwn,
so vanished Gwawl no more to be seen.
Married that day were Pwyll and his wife,
never again to be put through such strife.

It is said that on the evening of that happy day,
a hagged old man limped through the fray,
though no one knew who this old master had been,
by the morning the bag and the old man weren't seen.

One Legged Pete

One Legged Pete

This poem started off one morning as a play on words as to what it means to be legless. In other words drunk as a skunk or as they say in fashionable society inebriated (sic). Anyway being Andrew I thought that I would take the play on words ones step further. One step beyond. In fact one step too many. So here we have one legged Pete. One step too far!

One Legged Pete

One legged Pete worked for the man,
hammering wood to panel a van,
and even though slow he did a good job,
when banging away he didn't seem odd.
His bad leg was walnut he made it himself,
an old piece he found on top of the shelf,
he cut and sanded and planed it down fine,
then fitted it on and strapped it with vine.
Hopping round town with one leg of wood,
he stripped it all off to show Miss Good,
showing how fine the grain was to see,
when polished so well with wax from a bee.
But the woman she screamed for to see Pete hop,
and pushed him in fear then called for a cop,
the police came around and arrested old Pete,
for exposing himself with one leg so neat.
So shouting inanely they stole his wood leg,
for evidence of all this weird man had said,
and hopping round town on one leg alone,
Pete felt angry and so headed home.
Charged for exposure indecent they say,
so one leg only is how he'll stay.
The evening sun sinks so alone,
and old Pete hops with one leg of bone.
Never again to be with two,
for his broken heart; was torn right through.
The lesson to learn from this sad tale is clear,
don't bother to slave to be better and dear,
just sup up your beer then order some more,
one leg or two don't matter you bore!

The Bongle Beat

The Bongle Beat

The Bongle Beat is an imaginery dance craze. Maybe a bit Afro western. Maybe a few kettle drums. Maybe a little grinding electric guitar. Always with a strong manic beat. Always frantic and always street culture though.

The Bongle Beat

For the Bongle Beat we beat bass time,
that's a hit for you and a bash for mine,
Bongling boldly brashly thrashed,
bashing drum and symbols crashed.
Oh Bongle me and Bongle free,
bouncing Bongle beat to be,
Bongle me both near and far,
briskly Bongle for all you are.
Bongle me and beat time call,,
manic Bongle one and all,
when all know Bongle freely see,
the Bongle bangle bouncing key.
Freefall Bongle beat the time,
true felt Bongle rhythm mine,
in times of old they had no doubt,
wind the bass and start to shout,
wave your hands and hit the beat,
Bongle's " IN " so hit the street.

Father Thames - Fog of 1988

Father Thames - Fog of 1988

In pagan times Londoners used to assign a spirit God name to the meandering serpent like trawl of the favourite river in London. It is said that this could have originally been taken from an older deity such as Poseidon, the Greek God of the Sea, or maybe some earlier Egyptian God of the Seas. Who knows!

People can be homeless for a variety of reasons. Sometimes this is permanent and sometimes this is temporary for people who are between one stage of life and another in some way. In summer 1988 I witnessed life by the side of the banks of the River Thames for a short while. Meths drinkers, people so far gone from drinking meths that they were barely human beings anymore. Stabbings, and people falling to their deaths into the Thames whilst intoxicated. I will always remember the constant sound of the flow of the waves of the Thames. Also the sound and smell and warmth of a down and out's warm fire. It is striking that the real culture of London often does not reveal itself until an experience like this occurs. The maritime culture that hides beneath, and still persists in some ways, the sharp pressed briskness of the business community. Everything else is just bling!

FATHER THAMES INTRODUCING HIS OFFSPRING TO THE FAIR CITY OF LONDON
(A Design for a Fresco in the New Houses of Parliament)

Father Thames - Fog of 1988

Old Father Thames stood proud and grand,
Poseidon's trident right there in his hand,
and how the fog calls the meandering flow,
serpent like river so few really know.

Murmuring people call all around,
the drinks flowed smoothly and songs came out loud,
singing along by the banks of high tide,
A fire it glowed so it's warmth scorched my hide.

Now the swaying drinks caught the ripple of night,
one such fell in dying in fright,
but the ebb and the flow it whispered it's sound,
they tried to find him the corpse ne'r found.

In such a night time the waves praise the stars,
whilst lost souls gather far from all cars,
swirling of waves and the fog now does grow,
no home had they just stars that did show.

Reflections on waves sent by old Thames,
our father for all flows round the bends,
bending on by the serpent like trawl,
seen in the distance it echoes to all.

Old Father Thames guard me these nights,
without a bed I sleep here in fright,
by the banks of the Thames here I stay,
cardboard boxes warm me this day.

Lying and listening to the singing of tide,
commotions and drunks shout whilst I hide,
the glint of a knife and the swigging of meths,
reduce folk to nothing and nothing is left.

A shout and a scream and a man he falls,
screaming and running a woman she calls,
her partner lies his life seeps till bled,
why did he come was he out of his head?

Still those gathered sing where they sit,
warmed hands by fire and cider they hit,
weathered are eyes and they turn to the sky,
till night time and fog denies those who spy.

Oh Father of night time and Father of sea,
watch over us now and keep us all free,
the flow of life and the circling times,
flow as one as Big Ben now chimes.

Afterglow From The Tenth

Afterglow From The Tenth

So so many cities have a culture that revolves around high rise living. For those that have never hung about around a city, or lived in a high rise block, it is very much an unknown cultural existence. Life is not the same from a high rise block. It's not better, it's not worse, it's just different.

Some naive folk say "how could people live like that!" This is in some ways ignorance because ignoring social benefit type blocks; it is often a personal choice to adopt/adapt high rise living as a personal option. Indeed in many cities of the world high rise living is the norm and far from the exception. The high rise block is one of the main factors in the way in which modern city street culture has developed and is a quintessential part of it.

Afterglow From The Tenth

When morning light finds you there,
wrapped as one without a care,
we are two and two are one,
till dawn light bids you off and gone.

Our bodies pressed your curves so fine,
how could they know you'd end up mine?,
your long dark hair falls to the sheet,
now fades the glow that sparked the heat.

Entwined as one with heart beat timed,
for all that was we longed and pined,
but breakfast time brings busy doubts,
out on the street the new day shouts.

For now our afterglow brings highs,
as getting dressed starts morning sighs,
stretching as the world awakes,
and morning traffic roars and shakes.

Somewhere up above and far,
sky scraped sky line 'neath a star,
starts to rise the dawning light,
high rise life and concrete sight.

Bustles, shouts, and morning calls,
we; way above the market stalls,
now tenth floor finds the morning greets,
and I close the door to hit the streets.

Reflections of Time

Reflections of Time

Some people like to reflect on the passage of time. I don't. I find no joy in the pastime of looking back on yesteryear and praising it for what it was what so ever. Largely because I live for the future and prefer to live for those who are futuristic. The past is what I am built of. Brick by brick. But the future is the final product that is finished and complete.

References to Charon in the poem relate to the ferry boatman over the river to the after life Kingdom of Hades.

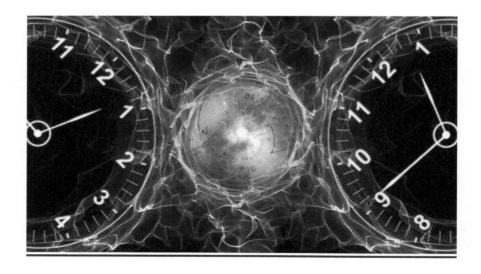

Reflections of Time

Don't cry for me if the wind blows through my soul,
it whistles sweetly of the times gone by it stole,
times of love and times of strife and hate,
still it blows as cobwebs tear our fate.

Don't feel distressed if my eyes show flames of old,
they burn so fiercely but all inside is cold,
all the plans that we presume to set,
burn to cinders for time does not regret.

Fret you not if I frown to see your face,
so many years I could but fall from grace,
your beauty was truly all I felt inside,
a presence of soul not fears to hide behind.

Cry not for me when I meet my final call,
and Charon trawls the waters as I fall,
what worth sees he to my shattered self gone by,
so I return and strive to fly so high.

Not me my friend all old fights have gone,
a darkened book of photos; yes once they shone,
but too old are they and waves of time now flow,
no one to see or resurrect their glow.

Let me sit and sip the wine of youth,
I'll reinvent and come right back as proof,
bother me not with times that have now flown,
let me fly with schemes so new as shown.

Æthelred the Unready

Æthelred the Unready

Æthelred the Unready was one of the youngest dark age kings of England. He was granted the throne of England at the age of twelve. He was named the "unready" as a pun. This being because he was so well advised that he knew everything that was going on, everywhere, from the service of his court advisors at the palace.

When Æthelred came to be King there was a relatively peaceful period with Denmark. But I dare say that the Danish interpreted a twelve year old King as being weak as a person; so Danish raiding parties started to attack all parts of England again a few years later.

Æthelred the Unready

Æthelred the Unready,

was oh so steady,

when given the throne of England at twelve

Well advised since 978,

and son of Edgar his life was great,

life was peaceful right at the start,

till Denmark broke the peace in his heart.

In the 980's Denmark hit him sore,

when the Battle of Malden changed the score,

Æthelred paid Denmark to stay away,

with tribute in Danegeld sent their way.

Æthelred the Unready,

was oh so steady,

when given the throne of England at twelve.

In 1002 on Saint Brice's Day,

Æthelred attacked all Danes on his way,

to the band of settlements all around,

and all Danes were slaughtered were ever found.

Now in the hordes on St Brice's day,

slaughtered and screaming where they lay,

one was Gunhilde daughter of Sweyn,

and there she lay and died in pain.

Æthelred the Unready,

was oh so steady,

when given the throne of England at twelve.

Had not Æthelred killed a Royal,

England would have won for their toil,

but Sweyn the father owned Denmark's throne,

and he swore to kill till England he owned.

So setting forth to England's coast,

a manic band from Denmark's host,

and slain were all who stood their ground,

till Sweyn was King of all he found.

Æthelred the Unready,

was oh so steady,

when given the throne of England at twelve.

Æthelred ran in fear for his life,

to Normandy's shore and away from strife,

and in Normandy he sat for the final stand,

waiting for news from his loyal band.

Then news it came but later on,

as Sweyn he died and the throne was won,

as Æthelred marched on England's fields,

retaking the throne and all it yields.

Æthelred the Unready,

was oh so steady,

when given the throne of England at twelve.

<u>Life</u>

Life

Life. What is life for? Does life need a purpose or it enough that it exists without questioning why it exists? I exist therefore I am. Extant life is life. It doesn't need a raison detre. Live it.

Life

Life flows like a river in time,

you have your space and I have mine,

but sometimes if our paths should meet,

then you know how our life's complete,

how many really ever know,

the right one in life who'll really show,

the love so true and oh so rare,

and when then found how people stare,

for two as one of sharing soul.

and two as one complete as whole,

a treasure to find of single mind,

oh joy in simple tasks to bind,

but how so few that know the truth,

of love's long trail and utter proof,

most just see what comes their way,

n'er to know how lovers play,

never to know the oneness of soul,

the rarest find that once they stole.

days may come and days pass by, but the flame burns
on deep inside.

With Ale We Sail

With Ale We Sail

I have been a real ale fan since I can first remember visiting pubs. Theakstons Brewery, Shepherd Neame Brewery, Firkin, Spitfire, Old Peculiar, Pedigree, Bishops Finger, Kentish Ale. In fact any word, or phrase, that is part of the real ale vernacular is something that I have seriously studied. Seriously studied at one time or another since first starting work. Normally whilst sitting on a bar stool! This is a limerick for a change.

With Ale We Sail

When seeking the best pint of ale,
whilst searching both hill and dale,
malt and hops,
the flow never stops,
till all of us lie rather pale.

Towards a Distant Horizon

Towards a Distant Horizon

Well there had to be a poem, somewhere in this book, that mirrors the title of the book. So here it is. A little piece of prose poem all wrapped up and ready to read. Just few thoughts scattered over the page....erm; well here it is "Towards a Distant Horizon!".

Towards a Distant Horizon

Long journey ahead. I long to know the way.
Heading to a distant time that somehow, somewhere,
holds my destiny. Just there beyond! Beyond a hill?
Beyond a valley? Or just beyond?

A way ahead where the sun shines brightly way
beyond the golden fields. Where the birds swoop then
rise and flock as one until flapping in the distance
they too are gone.

A horizon. A new horizon. Not an end but a beginning.
A new horizon arising somewhere, some place,
sometime!

So I'll pack my bags and wander far. Following on
where the birds call loudly from the distance and the
crows mock in wheat waving fields along the way. The
road meanders but the destination is straight.

Somewhere way ahead. In the distance. Just some
where. I'm sure to know when I've found it. Just
somewhere way ahead; and I travel so long, till finally
I will find it. Or perhaps it finds me?

Winter Solstice

Winter Solstice

The Winter Solstice, or Hibernal Solstice, is simply the shortest day of the year. A time of year when following the shortest day every day gets longer, there is more sun light and the whole planet starts to turn anew and revive. In ancient Greek mythology the Moon is Selene. In Egyptian Lah. Whilst the Equinox is really about the position of the sun; worship of the moon and planets and stars was always a normal behaviour during the solstice in older pastoral religions . An Equinox is the moment in which the plane of Earth's equator passes through the center of the Sun's disk which occurs twice each year.

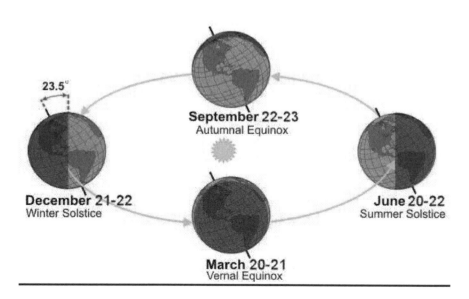

23.5°

September 22-23
Autumnal Equinox

December 21-22
Winter Solstice

June 20-22
Summer Solstice

March 20-21
Vernal Equinox

Winter Solstice

See the planets spinning round,
joyful to the fanfare sound,
praise be to the moon in flight,
Equinox or Solstice night.
Sing along to the darkest time,
comets all and skies sublime,
winter Solstice shortest day,
brings a change that's here to stay.
Shortest day of Equinox,
Clouds that burst with joy because,
a change from old to new now starts
days grow longer darkness parts.
Praise the moon in silver flight,
Equinox on darkest night,
Selene or Lah your name's are known,
now change the world and move alone.
Capricorn's Tropic here to see,
northern hemisphere to be,
now let the sun inch by degree,
peel the bells and set us free.
Free to dance with star gaze time,
the cosmic interstellar rhyme,
shortest day and time of change,
praise the Sun in aura strange.
Winter Solstice circle round,
gather with the babbling crowd,
way below the Christmas lights,
Solstice days and Solstice nights.
Sing the song of cosmic flight,
strike up the band with all your might,
dancing, shouting, revelry,
Selene or Lah our moon time be.

Go Lightly

Go Lightly

Go lightly is a farewell in meaning. It means fair thee well, or take care pal, or steady as you go, or even may you go in peace. Take your pick which ever meaning you wish.

This poem, however, is about a surreal scene by a lakeside. A peaceful place not to be disturbed too greatly. A place of the magic of the firefly and the fairy light left out at night to guide home the water vole.

Go Lightly

Go lightly from the dell where the firefly light the way by star gazing minions. Watch that the moon still beams and praise the sparkling of rippling night time currents of the lake. Glowing by the light of Cygnus and Aquilla themselves above.

Oh the moon! Smile down upon us with your golden aura. Pushing tiny stars away upon your darkened flight. The flight of your timeless face only overshadowed by eternal omnipresence.

Now step lightly and cross the waters slowly. As trees whisper to you in soft wind flared voices of the very days you had forgotten to remember. Whispering carefully, and quietly, while field mice stir from slumber. Then the reeds part to the splash of a tiny water vole looking to see who is approaching.

Go lightly my friend; for tomorrow is another day. Go lightly and allow the dark night sky to ease your time into the encroaching new day's beginning. Go lightly!

Spam Me Up

Spam Me Up

I wrote Spam me Up in the hope that I could get the UK/USA Spam manufacturing company to use it as part of their marketing for Spam products. In fact it was submitted to their commercial campaigns marketing department. I was always a big fan of the Spam Spam Spam sketch by Monty Python's Flying Circus so I have always fancied writing my own sequel. As with all Spam related literature, and adverts, and poetry, and songs, it is completely non-serious. ;)

Spam Me Up

Spam and chips for me for tea,
don't complain it's yours from me,
of all the Haute Cuisine we know,
spam and chips and hot "to go".
Sizzling in it's batter coat,
spam is king right down "yu'r throat",
spam served hot for spam has shown,
down through time it's spam we've known.
Spam for me and nicely sliced,
or in a bun with pickles diced,
spam n' rice or chopped in stew,
spam I love it's surely true ?
Spam for breakfast with an egg,
eat it up don't be a "smeg",
if all the famous known ate spam,
they'd all show true in all they "am".
Spam of old and spam of new,
spam for lunch oh spam so true,
spam is surely all I feel,
spam is winning every deal.
Give me spam and don't be boring,
without me spam you'd leave me snoring,
a world without me spam would sigh,
without me spam I'd surely die.
Spam n' beans and n' chips n' bread,
spam me up and fill me 'ead,
before the dawn of spam there was,
no known spam at all to because?
Now the evening dusk time draws,
spam is with me safe indoors,

frying, splurting, browning spam,
tells me who I really am.
Spam to me is all I know,
without me spam it's time to go,
spam me up and hit the chips,
spam for all so shake yer hips!

A Cinquain for Christmas

A Cinquain for Christmas

Every now and then I like a change from prose poems and, standard rhyming poetry, and epic rhymes. Everyone knows that I like to do the odd limerick and the odd cinquain here and there. It's all about keeping poetry fun. Poetry is a people's art form that belongs with folk culture. It doesn't belong in a dark book case gathering dust with the musty smell of yester year. It belongs to the people and is for the people. That is where poetry belongs. Adelaide Crapsey used to have great fun when the very first Cinquain was invented and that is what poetry is for. It is for fun.

A Cinquain for Christmas

Yule Tide,
good will season,
Christmas good cheer to all,
fairy lights guide the way for all,
to call.

Lunch Time Pangs

Lunch Time Pangs

The time in life when I most enjoyed lunch was when I was running a property management and lettings agency in Birmingham City, UK. Driving around from one appointment, to another, spaced about one ever forty minutes generates a real hunger. Whether it was meeting somebody at a pub for lunch or just sitting in a filling station car park with a stack of newly bought triangular cut sandwiches; lunch was a hit. Lunch was IT!

Yule Tide,

Lunch Time Pangs

Lunch time,
it's crunch time,
oh happy little munch time.

Burgers and beans you know what it means,
fried egg and ham I don't give a damn,
steak pie and mash I'll give it a thrash.

Lunch time,
it's crunch time,
oh happy little munch time.

Bagels and jam forget who I am,
Pizza and fries give me the highs,
kippers and peas I'm down on my knees.

Lunch time,
it's crunch time,
oh happy little munch time.

It's chicken curry so what's the hurry,
samosa and rice at least once or twice,
a plate full of these with fried egg and cheese.

Lunch time,
it's crunch time,
oh happy little munch time.

Onions and mince & a jelly with quince,
Plaice beans and chips with boiled egg for dips,
kebabs all day and I promise I'll stay.

Lunch time,
it's crunch time,
oh happy little munch time.

Feed me lunch!...............

Life - A Pre Planned Journey

Life - A Pre Planned Journey

Astronomers and scientists say that everything in space works in cyclical form and never in a straight line. In other words if a space craft sets out to try to fly in a straight line, faster than the speed of light even maybe, then in reality it will have flown in a curve when observed. Some say that if one tries to fly in a straight line for far enough, maybe even several billion light years at high speed, then eventually one would come back to the point that one first started at. In other words one would re pass the planets originally seen at the start of the journey. Because everything in space works in elliptical circles and never in straight lines. Perhaps time works in circles as well? WE always assume that we are born and set out in life in a straight line as we age and time progresses. Perhaps that isn't true? If time works in circles, as well as space, then everything that we do has already been done before because there is no beginning and no end. Only a circle of space and a circle of time! A re living of everything within our circle of time that has already happened before; and will happen again. Spooky! What a thought! Lol……

Life - A Pre Planned Journey

Life came with sunrise and a baby's young cry,
glowing with power of a new life's try,
then quickly life grew with a twist and a change,
for all of the ageing and yearning in range,
Then all of the mornings and night times passed,
time seemed to tease in all that it tasked,
sunrise and sunset and cloudy old skies,
swift were the days and oh I despise.
Despise the swiftness of time's sweet decay,
so let me soar high away from the fray,
faster than light now free my soul,
speeding passed stars and planets whole,
let me fly by the fading of life,
let me beat time and scupper it's strife,
I see decay in the twilight of days,
of those that I knew and swore that I'd praise,
As numbers now dwindle I swear in a cry,
hold me back not and don't even try,
I glory not at the fading of page,
not time nor death; shall you keep me caged.

Sunday Morning

Sunday Morning

Sunday mornings. That lazy day when it doesn't matter how long one stays in bed as there will never be a complaint. A nice simple poem about Sunday mornings.

Sunday Morning

Sunday morning bell call chimes,
bird call songs and garden times,
sunday news and pillows doze,
sunrise streaks and breeze that blows.

See the flowers nod their heads,
secret knowledge in their heads,
of all those sleepy sunday morns,
choicest snooze that no one scorns.

Eyelids open wearily,
let me sleep till I can see,
clang the tea cups morning tea,
smell that toast so buttered free.

What are sundays really for?
question not just lie and snore,
for sunday morning not to think,
leave the washing in the sink,
and doze till morning brings around,
sunday blessings all have found.

Behold the Sea

Behold the Sea

I think I was maybe inspired by some old album I once heard by he Waterboys for the title of this one.
For those who don't know the Waterboys were an Irish folk/rock band. Still on the go at the time of writing I believe. Fascinating thing the sea. Almost hypnotises if you stare at the ebb and the flow for too long.

Behold the Sea

Where the seagulls cry so let my soul roam,
where the cliffs are high let the sea surf moan,
and blue sky gaze to the distance far,
where night time gave rest to a star,

For the fish shoals spin in a group as one,
in the deepest depths with the mermaid's song,
and Neptune struck with his trident true,
as barques sailed round with sailors few.

The stony beach of pebbles combed,
for the star fish reached in the rock pool honed,
here sits the throne of the sea King's home,
as Urchins cry for the waves alone.

Lashing and roaring with the high tide's height,
as Herring swim to the Dolphin's delight,
and Mackeral play way down out of view,
as seaweed sways as if in a queue.

The murky depths of the Ocean's depth,
saw crabs that crawl and dance in step,
dancing for the waves that sing with the tide,
for the song of creation and the sea bed that hides.

Dark Night

Dark Night

Another nice little cinquain here. A Cinquain about a dark night time.

This is a Cinquain poem (pronounced Sin-Cain). This is a type of poem first invented by Adelaide Crapsey around 100 years ago in the USA. The Cinquain has set rules as to how it should be written:-

* Cinquain poems must be 5 lines long.
* A Cinquain poem has 2 syllables on the first line, 4 on the second, 6 on the third, 8 on the 4th, and 2 syllables on the 5th line.
* Cinquain poems do not need to rhyme but can if you want.

Dark Night

Dark night,
I rest in grace,
star trail haze now in sight,
silver moon now light up my face,
so bright.

Just Three Old Monkeys

Just Three Old Monkeys

In the west the rise of New Age philosophy has led to the adoption of a variety of cultural influences in the Uk and the USA. One of these is the imagery of the three wise monkeys of ancient Japan and ancient China. The three wise monkeys of the East are also known collectively as Sanbiki. They each in turn represent:-

* See no evil.
* Hear no evil
* Speak no evil.

The names of the three monkeys are Mizaru, Kikazaru and Iwazaru. These being see no, hear no and speak no respectively. The philosophy of the three monkeys comes from a variety of early sources including the teachings of Confucius in the 4th century BC. The three monkeys are also seen to represent the Sanshi, or Holy Trinity of ghosts/corpses, that are said to inhabit each human being. It is said that every 60 days the Sanshi report to Ten Tei, or the Heavenly being, as to the bad deeds of people on earth. They are then judged on the basis of the report from Sanshi.

Just Three Old Monkeys

In ancient Japan and China long back,
came three wise monkeys and there they sat,
Mizaru, Kikazaru and Iwazaru were they,
Sanbiki to judge and share the way.

Commit no evil said Mizaru most grand,
hiding his eyes with the palms of his hands.
let not the foulness shadow my soul,
I will not see such bad things you stole.

Kikazaru will not hear you his ears are shut,
speak not so harshly and watch your foot,
for Sanshi knows all of your troubled life,
curse you no more of troubles and strife.

Iwazaru will not tell you,
the evilness that's true,
his mouth is tightly sealed,
for all you have to do.

For Ten Tei knows of your sordid ways,
and Sanshi will tell of your evil days,
let not you think that you've concealed,
all of your deeds with some sort of shield.

Think not and hear not and speak not too,
to purify your soul; through and through,
for Sanbiki know; and at the end of the day,
your judgment is coming when out of this fray.

Just a Thought - Lost in Time and Space

Just a Thought - Lost in Time and Space

Where do we roam to when first we cease to be alive? Is it that we just cease? Or is it that a ball of pure energy vacates our body seeking where to be and how to get to it's next existence? That is what this poem is about. The search of the inner soul and the search of lost love.

Just a Thought - Lost in Time and Space

I sense her still in the darkness of early hours. Somehow our souls entwined and wound around as one. The Yin and the Yang ; two halves of the sky. Out there somewhere but drawing on me like a silken thread. Memories of caress, of warmth, of fun. Nothing of that now. Just a dim sense of presence somewhere out there. In the darkness of a cloudy world.

The past haunts me not; it just draws me near. Drawing and sucking on my memories until each one becomes a chain to drag me back to the one that I once belonged.

Memories or chains? The faintly burning remnant of our flame burns inside me. Once it was strong; now just flickering. The flickers make me yearn for the first day that the flame was lit.

Then steadily sleep takes me away to a far distant land. Then, and only then, the flame inside lies forgotten; extinquished by successive rolling waves of sleep. Tomorrow will come when tomorrow will come. For now may the mists of night time darkness drag me away; so far far away.

Who Do You Think You Are?

Who Do You Think You Are?

What is this poem about? It's about a guy that everyone of us has met. He stands on the corner of the street or in your local pub or bar. He knows everything about everything but if you want him to do something for himself he can't. Because he doesn't really know how to do anything, at all, without making a mess of it.

This is the guy who won't stop talking incessantly about things he knows nothing about. This is the guy who will tell you exactly why you are doing everything wrong; but not have a clue as to how to do anything himself.

Who Do You Think You Are?

Did I ask you for your opinion all,
do I need your time to call,
did I say I need your thoughts on wings,
do I need such time to brawl?

Who the Hell do you think you are,
I haven't asked you for your view so far,
have I said I want your whole life's view,
I'd rather you choke you've blocked the queue.

Did I ask you for your opinion all,
do I need your time to call,
did I say I need your thoughts on wings,
do I need such time to brawl?

Did I say I like you and if so when,
what are you on about it's not even ten,
clear off home and ear ache someone else,
I don't want your verbal so leave it on the shelf.

Did I ask you for your opinion all,
do I need your time to call,
did I say I need your thoughts on wings,
do I need such time to brawl?

Here he comes over with even more advice,
I've told you once to shove it and stop being pseudo nice,
why do you think the folk all make way,
you bore their fried brains crazy with you there's no delay.

Did I ask you for your opinion all,
do i need your time to call,
did I say I need your thoughts on wings,
do I need such time to brawl?

Oh for some silence from the likes of Mr. bore,
I've told you oh so often it's eating at my core,
go back to your hutch & don't let the verbals out,
and take your words with you before I scream and shout.

Did I ask you for your opinion all,
do I need your time to call,
did I say I need your thoughts on wings,
do I need such time to brawl?

Creeping up slow with his advice line for the day,
sorry bud I've things to do I couldn't stand to stay,
your wife she's gone and left you and your kids they don't call
round,
can't you see it's you they need to cease the tripe you've found.

Did I ask you for your opinion all,
do I need your time to call,
did I say I need your thoughts on wings,
do I need such time to brawl?

Far From the Bland Lands

Far From the Bland Lands

Back in the 1800's a little lady ended up living in the west country moors on her own. She was in her twenties. This was after her family's new world migration, from previous centuries, went badly and she had to return to Britain alone from Canada.

She returned on her own by ship from Canada and spent the entirety of her life on the west country moors with no money; apart from one day when she discovered some coins to spend in a town. She was so delighted that she wrote a poem about her experience of actually visiting shops.

Visiting shops, for one day in her life only, was the highlight of her whole life. Her adventure started by the building of a very small coracle boat to cross the river to the town over the water. She made the very small coracle boat in an unusual way with a stretched cowhide nailed around it to make it water tight because this was one of the materials available to her on the moors. The hide rotted, as the river she crossed was the estuary to the Ocean and it is full of salt which rots animal hide down when dried.

The Victorian era local authorities of the area had her prosecuted for owning a water born vessel that was not up to regulations in it's manufacture and design. She never crossed the river to the town on the horizon , over the water, again.

Far From the Bland Lands

From Canada she came to the moorland bland,
black long hair once tied with a band,
to a pretty abode all stone in the fields,
and there she stayed as her life so revealed.

The bland land moor was oh so alone,
but fair well did she and never did moan,
at the solitude of a moorland day,
till one summer some man came that way.

A woodland copse and a bird call song,
while the river flowed on to the estuary strong,
way in the distance a far river shore,
across the wide flow where the tide pulls your oar.

There at the cottage she built a small boat,
and sealed it with hide with wonder to float,
wonder craft to cross the river so wide,
while she sat there waiting the right time of tide.

Then so far from bland lands she crossed the swell,
to see the distant harbour so well,
and there to seek out a less lonely place,
with shops and Inns with a cheeriest face.

But so wild was she with a moorland fate,
and though she found truly good things that she ate,
return then did she to her wildest bland land,
on that little craft for the river that spanned.

Some say what a saddest of life,
deeply the wildest of moorland strife,
but forever on would she recall,
those shops, and inns, and the spending in all.

One day in her life she ventured on,
to visit a town where her fortune shone,
the memory of one day in her life,
to spend and drink and not feel such strife.

As the sun sank down on her bland land home,
she smiled at the thought of not being alone,
somewhere a town on that far distant shore,
a place where she once spent time in a store.

When one day at last a child she bore,
daughter of some man she'd seen there before,
she knew she'd one day tell of that day,
when she strayed across the wide river's spray,
and visited shops in the boat that she spanned,
covered in hide and just as she'd planned.

Girl at the Window

Girl at the Window

For about a year I had a blonde haired female, for some reason sitting in her bedroom window at night with the curtains wide open every evening and the light on in a property quite close by. Not a prostitute I might add; just somebody who wanted to sit being "visible" at the window in the evening. It always fascinates me as to what drives people to do odd things in life.

Anyway it reminded me, in some way, of some sort of modern day Lady of Shallot (Tennyson). Eventually she just vanished, left the area, and the lit bedroom window went on to be curtained, shut, and dark every evening.

Girl at the Window

As dark draws in now there she fits,
with golden hair so long it sits,
upon her waist and hips so curved,
as with the breeze it blows and swerves.

Seen in a window from beyond,
and every night time so belonged,
no curtains drawn and there we saw,
no shyness of who stare before.

Like some last vision a lady seen,
Shallot's own tale a lady's dream,
but not Shallot this modern pose,
and who knows why or who she knows.

Sitting at the window true,
waiting for only who knows who,
but how she grieves to be observed,
by those who pass the pavements kerb.

But then one day the room stayed dark,
in the night time with no spark,
of the image of this lady true,
no mirage of this beauty's view.

With curtains drawn and blinds now shut,
and darkness drowned the image cut,
so who was she and what was there?
To make her want to sit and stare.

The curtains wide for all those nights,
her beauty of ephemeral sights,
so awhile she sat and now no more,
Shallot's dream has left our shore,
and darkness holds upon this place,
with curtains drawn no more that face.

Give Me a Break Dude

Give Me a Break Dude

I have reached the stage in life that I now find when ever I get a sales pitch, tricky dicky, salesperson, con artist, or other such schemer I can read what they are doing before they do it. It's experience in life. very simple.

This poem is dedicated to all the slick, sick, schemers, and wheeler dealers, and all the crooked contracts that I have never signed.

Give Me a Break Dude

Don't mince my dreams with drivel and spam,
I don't need you here let me be who I am,
you think you're clever with schemes you've planned,
I see right through so you be damned.
Don't give me a sales pitch outside my door,
I know "where you're at" I've told you before,
Mr. Slick leave; don't tread on my floor,
oh; Two tongued Tessie just like before.
Lord; don't suck my brain I can't stand your pitch,
maybe it's me should leave; I've got that itch,
get out of my brain with your dim dreams and play,
I'll head for a new land and a life to stay.
Swell worded Dave keep your script away,
two faced Carol may you rot n' decay.
sick slink Pete try to keep it neat,
bad faced Kim just admit defeat.

The In Crowd (life in a jam jar)

The In Crowd (life in a jam jar)

In or out? Trendy or not trendy? Ultra fashion or just
dé modé? These are questions that some people feel to
be important. The need to fit is sometimes infectious
and even if one feels the need to not fit that is the
same thing. A desire to not fit in is counter culture.
Counter culture has just as many followers as high
fashion. Hence you are still segregating yourself into
a cultural sub group by rejecting "IN" crowd fashions
and trends. That's what this poem is about.

The In Crowd (life in a jam jar)

In crowd, out crowd, any old crowd?
Is it rather trendy, or just rather loud?

Arm in arm up the hill, always on the mall,
tight jeans, strobe thrills, drinking with a pal.

Trending new phase style, too cool to high five,
fashion right posing, street style for a drive.

Top down, tailed back, latte at the Den,
the smell of fresh coffee, blending down again.

Shows and films, Cinema, glossed up nice and big,
strutting by bill boards, then off to see a gig.

car horns and buses, cross the road at Bates.
Taxi rides crawling, clicking up the rates,

In or out or demode? Fashion at the core?
Fast life street scene, what's it all been for?

Garden Birds

Garden Birds

We always love the birds in my home. Feed them every day and they've just scratched to pieces a two year old bird bath; so I'm having to arrange for a new, more solid, one so that they don't do it again this month. Anyway garden birds is what this poem is all about.

Garden Birds

How they come from all around,
a flap of the wing and a squawking sound,
peanuts left and fat balls too,
a little bread and see what they do.
Robins, and Magpies, and Starlings flock,
Black Birds, and Thrushes, and Blue Tits, take stock,
of how some splash in the bird bath all,
then wing to the air with a loudest of call,
Pigeons peck at the seed there on,
Doves descend but quickly are gone,
to and throw birds eat then depart,
returning again as the Sparrows now dart.
Sitting in trees surveying the scene,
tweeting and pecking and fighting so keen,
circling around now even more come,
a veritable meal till all is now done.
Lined on fences and roof tops they perch,
one on the shed and more in a Birch,
looking and squabbling and flying around,
till all food is gone and they soar from the ground.
Such good friends at the start of rise,
first in the morn oh their breakfast they prize,
suet, and fat balls, and nuts galore,
till all now is gone so ends the furore.

Misogyny Keith

Misogyny Keith

I think most people have had a period in life when they have been a bit of a hell raiser and on the booze too much. The thing that is difficult, though, is going with the change of modern culture to some these days! Men as well as women are supposed to hit the pavement running when it comes to domesticity these days, In the year 2018. The ability to prepare food and do household chores! It isn't even an option to men anymore! Maybe before in previous decades it was an option to men!

Self sufficiency is a must for everyone nowadays. The use of a female to provide labour and provide all domestic labouring services, in the home, whilst a man sits doing nothing is one form of misogyny in the modern world. It is the same as having an unpaid human slave. In previous decades the thinking about this matter was different. Because in previous decades people did not follow the same form of culture. Everything is different now.

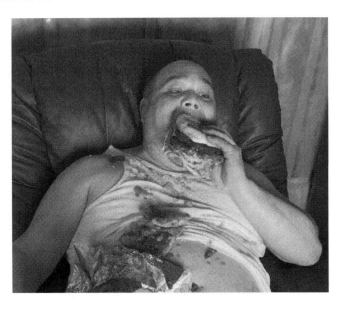

Misogyny Keith

Keith sat there with a spoon in his hand,
the reason why no one could stand,
with pans, and mixers, and plates all around,
but not a cooked meal could there be found.

Food in the freezer and there it will stay,
Keith on his own 'cause his wife went away,
so why should our Keith stand for to cook,
he'd rather go out to the pub for a look.

Why Cook at all?
It's oh such a bore,
let someone else; it's so much a drag!

The 'veggie rack' has rotted away,
the chips in the fryer went brown the last day,
the milk went sour and green with decay,
but he don't do "no cookin' " and that's how he'll stay.

He'd throw out old food that went bad if he could,
but the bins are full and he don't feel he should,
"why make a fuss when me wife'll be back!",
I'll open a beer it'll be such a crack.

Why cook at all?
it's oh such a bore,
let someone else; it's so much a drag!

There's misogyny Keith and things in the sink
" I don't do no washing I'd rather they stink!"
"Me wife 'll be back" said misogyny Keith,
"I'd do the washing but she'd call me a thief".

"A lass does the washing and cookin' for true",
"it aint me business cause I'm one of the few",
"I'll stick to me role created for man",
"It aint me fault it's the almighty plan!

Why cook at all?
it's oh such a bore,
let someone else; it's so much a drag!

"Nah! Men don't cook it's unmanly and grot!",
"as far as washing they'd call me a clot",
"till me wife come' home 'cause she misses the work",
"I'll not do no cookin' she'd call me a jerk.

So the old drips of ketchup all stain the floor,
" It aint my job to clean I've told yer before",
and Keith's belly grew as the sloth set in,
he'd lie on his back with a bottle of gin.

Why cook at all?
it's oh such a bore,
let someone else; it's so much a drag!

Maybe an eight pack of lager 'd be good,
gulp it down quickly just like you should,
"misogyny rules!" said Keith at the door,
swearing blind drunk it's what a man's for.

His belly so bloated so no one would chase,
this stupid old fool who became such a case,
waiting for dinner and his wife to arrive,
his heart finally faltered and there he died.

Why cook at all?
it's oh such a bore,
let someone else; it's so much a drag!

A Micro Cosmos within an Eye.

A Micro Cosmos within an Eye.

It is so so difficult to describe a feeling using either written words, because languages that we use are maybe still primitive in their descriptive ability, or indeed in paint on canvas. This is just a poem about personal memories of an old flame. Hence it is private really. Hope it works as a prose poem though. The feeling of looking in to a loved one's eye is the same as entering somebody's soul in some respects.

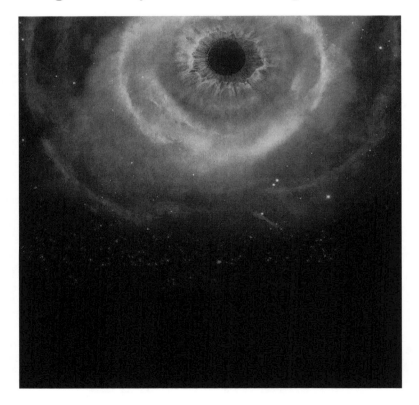

A Micro Cosmos within an Eye.

Back then a light shone in your eye. A sparkle of happiness. A light of success. A mirror of being and of self. Mostly a light of love.

A mirror of everything encapsulated within one little sparkle within your pupil. A little light of being capturing the essence of soul all the way back to the beginning of time.

So Sirius span round within the micro cosmic world of a single eye. Galaxies shine and spin within the millions of years of creation to produce that one spark; within an eye. A sparkle within your eye.

Yet still that spark was all I ever wanted to see. All I ever did see and all that ever brought happiness. A mirror of the cosmos within the micro cosmic essence and sparkle of an eye.

A macro cosmic marvel within a micro cosmic creation.

Proud Dingbat

Proud Dingbat

Well we have all heard about Dingbats I guess. Everybody knows what they are all about! But how many people can really say that they have ever either owned a Dingbat or had a Dingbat staying at home? It is questions like these that always produce a deathly silence. It is questions like these that motivated this poem. PROUD DINGBAT.

Proud Dingbat

I once had a Dingbat proud and tall,
and when we went out my name it would call,
standing there proud in the midst of the mall,
it weren't just a dingbat but really my pal.

Dingbats are tall but often so small,
curved but straight it depends on their fate,
my Dingbat did sing all of the while,
not any old bat and so full of style.

Dingbats walumpth all over the aisle,
when seen together they do it with guile,
hiding round pillars or maybe a hedge,
they dig up the garden and eat all your veg'.

Now if you are careful and feed them on spice,
they fall on your belly and tickle so nice,
Dingbats are clever in a slapstick way,
so keep them so treasured; and your Dingbat will stay.

Feed them on porridge at midnight sharp,
they don't need a spoon and it's best in the dark,
glumpfing flat footed they'll eat the whole bowl,
and fall on their backs almost full to the soul.

On fridays buy them a large carrot pie,
and watch how they dance to the clouds in the sky,
stomping around in a long Dingbat line,
but my Dingbat's at home; and with me, aye!

Now sing to the dawn of your Dingbat's day,
when it stomps around or gets lost in the hay,
for your Dingbat is here and you know it so true,
in a world without Dingbats there's nothing to do.

So There We Go

So There We Go

Well now. Folk attempting to write poetry always write about sublime scenes or surreal events. Or perhaps haughty hoity toity lofty words and descriptive paragraphs on the basis that uncle Fred bought them a Thesaurus for Christmas.

Well this poem is for the ordinary geezer standing at the bar. Is it a good poem? No; because writing about ordinary things is uninteresting and people prefer the sublime. The sublime with the haughty hoity toity lofty words instead ;)

So There We Go

So there we go said George at the bar,
it don't really matter who you are,
so there you go it's just one crowd,
in one door with the chickens loud.

Just one crowd of thought in here,
don't matter to think just a pint of beer,
if I had a thought I'd keep it right hid,
there's no place for thought and I never did.

Hiding in the crowd that seemed a tad loud,
but we've no great thoughts we're standing proud,
so there we go now just another great pint,
and some B & H I'll smoke 'em all night.

So there we go we're doin' right grand,
there's darts to do and another band,
a band that plays Abba like me uncle before,
and a trophy for the quiz a prize at the core.

There we go just another friday night,
a time to escape and get out of sight,
for the weekend stops; on sunday for sure,
don't kill me time out it's really a cure.

<u>Jurys Gap</u>

Jurys Gap

Jurys Gap is a small port, and rugged coast line, in East Sussex that was used by smugglers in previous centuries. It has a pebbled beach and is two miles away the marvellous yellow sands of Camber with it's golden sands and grassy dunes. It was used as a smugglers off loading point by both Jewish traders, from the middle east, and British smugglers. Inwards merchandise was subject to customs and excise duties if off loaded at Rye just along the coast. So Middle East traders, and smugglers alike, offloaded and hid their merchandise in the local pub, at Jurys Gap, in order to avoid paying Government duties on their exports.

Jurys Gap

Two miles away from Camber sands,
sits a bay pebbled where history stands,
by this smugglers pebbled whiskey soaked shore,
away from Rye where a fee was in store.

For smugglers from the Middle East found,
this haven stacked with no tax bound,
off loading foods, and jewels, and all that booze,
Jurys Gap was the port they'd choose.

No tax levied for boxes begot,
in Ye Olde Bell pub where hid they the lot,
and passages and tunnels below did they see,
from the pub to the point of the cargo so free.

So the gulls they screamed and the surf road strong,
and the wind and the rain battered so long,
for Jurys Gap sound of the pebbles in dark,
and the caskets and trunks unloaded full part.

Now the moon shines down with a grin,
on the cargo below with both rum and gin,
and bootleg whiskey from a distant shore,
far from the customs and excise score.

See through the window of Ye Olde Bell,
there sit the sailors who battled fair well,
through storm, and wave, and star lit night,
to reach this haven of smuggled delights.

Autumn in Flight

Autumn in Flight

I always get a kind of weird feeling when summer is over and autumn comes. It's something of a change in atmosphere that is unfathomable. Perhaps sudden change in barometric pressure? I really don't know. I always feel it as well as see it.

I love the browns and reds of autumn, as the leaves fall and gather. I also love the late autumn winds that scatter the falling leaves with a rustle all over the road. but that is about it. I am definitely a summer time person really.

Autumn in Flight

When the wind sounds within every crack round your door,

and teasing he whistles like never before.

Driving me out of my peaceful refrain,

as trees now bow to the bellowing rain.

Who ever said that autumn would come,

shutting old summer out till quite won.

Brown leaves that scatter reflected in light,

with yellows and golds of Autumn in flight.

The crisp crunch of leaves under my foot,

whirling around as the wind starts to rut.

Stabbing and taunting the Autumnal sky,

the clouds in a frenzy from their vantage on high.

The spirit of Autumn and death to renew,

new life from old and the green stems so true.

True to the cycle; this mystical flight,

the seasons own being within inner sight.

City Heat

City Heat

London City, Birmingham City, Coventry City, Leicester City, Nottingham City, New York City in the USA and others elsewhere in the world. I've happy memories of wandering around city landscapes in the burning city summer sun.

Bars and pubs, work contracts, trying not to be late, interviews, pin striped shirt and tie and driving around the same roads several times trying to find the right way to my destination. This is a city poem for a change.

City Heat

City heat throw me a breeze,
need some chill to stop this old wheeze!

Taxis pass by in the heat of midday,
smell of Kebabs and hi five all the way,
underground rumble from trains down below,
crowds hurry on like they've somewhere to go.

Commuters, computers, and old boys with cramps,
street scene drawings and street craze dance,
whizz 'em all round and dance your life away,
through to the evening this street dance play.

City heat throw me a breeze,
need some chill to stop this old wheeze!

Bars for stars and bars for Whisky Mac,
bottle neck beers and smokes all in a stack,
street side burgers and vans with ice cream,
shoe shine steady and rollin' like a dream.

Denim clad flirting all around the mall,
sunshine brings 'em looking for a pal,
and in centre square pigeons swoop the crowd,
landing in the fountain and cooing rather loud.

City heat throw me a breeze,
need some chill to stop this old wheeze!

Double decker buses and sectioned cycle lanes,
rattle of the coin falls and gurgle of the drains,
city beat soul never turn your face,
from those who truly follow and never lose the pace.

The glow of the city an aura seen from high,
seen from a distance all gold beneath the sky,
buzzing, and roaring, the frenetic city ways,
city whizz, and styling, frantic city days.

City heat throw me a breeze,
need some chill to stop this old wheeze!

End of the Day

End of the Day

The end of the day and the final poem of this book. Sit and open a bottle of wine. Just relax and watch the sun going down in a cloudless but darkening sky. Flick on the television and watch the news. Just relax and chill. Yes that's it ; just Chill!

End of the Day

Evening sinks to a darkened hue,
the day slows down as hours grow few,
birds in the distance call no more,
as the grasp of darkness closes the door.
The door of light on our daytime chores,
now firmly shut as the darkness scores,
lying still as a wall clock ticks,
counting the seconds; counting transfixed.
Voices chat in the distant streets,
laughing and joking under star lit greets,
the stars they swirl and spy from on high,
spy on us all from their vista nigh.
Thoughts of tomorrow and thoughts of today,
drifting on by as sleep shows the way,
the way to the morning and on to the dawn,
passing dream castles; on to sun born.

Acknowledgements

Acknowledgements

Poetry is an art form that was invented for the people and was originally by the people. Academics, and cultural pedants, can keep poetry classics from previous centuries on their dusty book shelves for as long as they want. The truth is that a glorious oral cultural tradition, such as poetry, does not belong in a University , or College, or Academic Journal.

Poetry belongs on the street where it was invented. For every academic spouting prose about the in depth meaning of some classic poem wording, written maybe 300 years ago, there is a little rhyme being formed on the pavement during a walk to work.

So long as poets such as Pam Ayres keep this oral tradition alive poetry will continue as a cultural norm. I developed an interest in publishing some of my poetry having been introduced to allpoetry.com. May people such as Kevin, the owner of Allpoetry.com, continue the good work of websites such as this for as long as can be.

It is all about keeping culture and art where they belong. Where they belong is on the street and with the people.

Lastly I must thank the community of Rushden, Northants, who have made my stay quiet, and undisturbed, enough for me to be able to complete this fourth book of poems.

Printed in Great Britain
by Amazon

85273479R00124